Action for the Environment

Clean Air

Rufus Bellamy

FRANKLIN WATTS
LONDON • SYDNEY

Franklin Watts
96 Leonard Street
London EC2A 4XD

Franklin Watts Australia
45–51 Huntley Street
Alexandria
NSW 2015

ISBN: 0 7496 5533 X

A CIP catalogue record for this
book is available from the
British Library

Printed in Malaysia

Editor: Adrian Cole
Design: Proof Books
Art Direction: Jonathan Hair
Picture Research: Kathy Lockley

Acknowledgements
ACDI/CIDA: 27 b. Joerg Boethling/Still Pictures: 15.
T. Bognar/Art Directors & TRIP Photo Library: 28.
Jon Bower/Ecoscene: 24. Andrew Brown/Ecoscene: 17 t.
DAS Fotoarchive/Still Pictures: 12. Digital Vision Ltd.
All rights reserved 25 b, 27 t. A. Doto/UNEP/Still
Pictures: 4. Julio Echart/Still Pictures: title page, 9.
Mark Edwards/Still Pictures: 14. Franklin Watts: 17 b,
25 t. Philippe Gontier/Science Photo Library: 20.
Greenpeace/Barry: 18, Greenpeace /Machalinek: 19 t,
Greenpeace /Van Capellen: 23. Chinch
Gryniewicz/Ecoscene: 10, cover tl. Robert Harding
Picture Library: 2, 5, 11 b, 31. Hulton Archive/Getty
Images: 6, 16. John Maier/Still Pictures: 13 t.
NASA/Science Photo Library: 19 b. Tony
Page/Ecoscene: 7 b, cover tr. N. Ray/Art Directors &
TRIP Photo Library: 13 b. Rex Features: 22, 26. Helene
Rogers/Art Directors & TRIP Photo Library: 21 b, 21 t.
Roland Seitre/Still Pictures: 8 b, cover b. Clyde H.
Smith/Still Pictures: 29. W. T. Sullivan III/Science
Photo Library: 8 t. A. Tovy/Art Directors & TRIP
Photo Library: 11 t. B. Turner/Art Directors &
TRIP Photo Library 7 t.

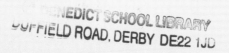

Contents

Air pollution action

Air pollution is one of the biggest environmental challenges we face. Millions of people breathe polluted air that is bad for their health. However, air pollution is a problem that can be solved.

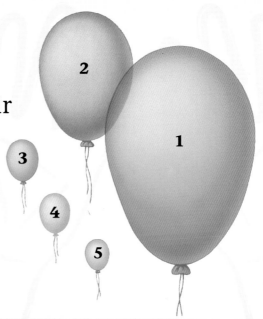

POLLUTED AIR

Air pollution is anything that makes the air unhealthy or that damages the atmosphere. Cars, factories and power stations are just some of the things that produce air pollution. It causes health problems that range from coughing to cancer. It also harms animals and plants and is even thought to be slowly heating up the Earth.

*Everyone should be able to breathe clean air. Air is made up of different gases: 78% nitrogen (**1**); 21% oxygen (**2**); and small amounts of argon (**3**), water vapour (**4**) and carbon dioxide (**5**).*

These children are taking part in an anti-air pollution protest. Despite world-wide activity to clean the air, studies show that over 1 billion people breathe air that is unhealthy.

AIR ACTION

Action is being taken to reduce air pollution worldwide. For example, dirty factories are being forced to clean up, cleaner transport schemes are being built and electricity is being produced in less-polluting ways. Despite these successes, many air pollution problems remain. But if everyone plays a part, they can be beaten.

We can all play a part in keeping the air clean. Bicycles such as this one produce no air pollution, unlike cars.

Action stations

Everyone can play a part in reducing air pollution. If you travel to school on foot or by bicycle, rather than in a car, you will stop some pollution being produced. Every year the average car produces about 4–5 tons of carbon dioxide — a gas that is thought to be warming the planet. Cars also produce chemicals, such as nitrogen oxides, that increase pollution.

Cleaning up a crisis

During the last century, as more people moved into cities and industry grew, air pollution caused many deaths. This made people take the problem seriously and a lot was done to clean the air.

LONDON SMOGS

One of the biggest disasters occurred in 1952 in London, UK, when air pollution from factories and fires produced a suffocating smog (a mixture of smoke and fog) that killed over 4,000 people. To solve the problem, people were only allowed to burn 'smokeless' fuels, such as coke or natural gas. However, these are fossil fuels, which still cause air pollution (see page 11).

The smogs in London, like this one, were so thick they were called 'pea-soupers'.

POLLUTION LAWS

In the second half of the 20th century, many countries introduced laws to combat air pollution. For example, in 1970 the USA passed the Clean Air Act. This law set limits on the amount of air pollution that factories, power stations and other sources of pollution could produce and played a central role in reducing pollution.

The Clean Air Act helped control air pollution in the USA. It meant that cities, such as Austin, Texas, shown here, remained pleasant places in which to live.

Action stations

In many countries, governments have banned lead in petrol because it is a major pollutant. Now in Europe, the USA and elsewhere, many cars are fuelled by lead-free or 'unleaded' petrol. Lead emissions have dropped dramatically since this happened – by over 90% in the USA. Where unleaded petrol is used, car emissions are no longer thought to be such a big health problem.

Filling up with unleaded petrol is not always possible. In many African cities, for example, unleaded petrol is much more expensive, and as a result lead emissions are up to ten times higher than those typical of European cities.

Pollution watch

All over the world, scientists monitor levels of air pollution. This work provides information about where the pollution comes from and what must be done to clean the air.

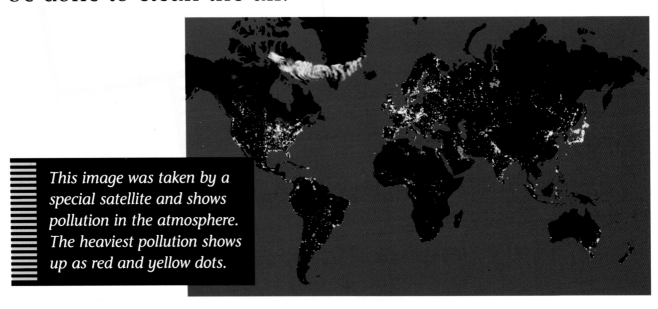

This image was taken by a special satellite and shows pollution in the atmosphere. The heaviest pollution shows up as red and yellow dots.

INVISIBLE ENEMY

Many pollutants are invisible gases. Scientists have to use pollution-monitoring equipment to find out how much pollution there is in the air. This equipment is placed on the ground and on buildings, and is carried by aeroplanes, balloons and satellites.

This pollution-monitoring device, attached to a balloon, is being released by a scientist in the Antarctic. Even remote places are not free from air pollution carried by the wind.

WARNING SIGNS

In many cities across the world, public warnings are given if air-monitoring machines detect that pollution has reached unhealthy levels. This allows people at risk, such as children who suffer from asthma, to stay indoors where they will be less affected.

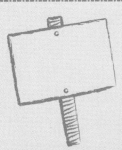

Action stations

Mexico City has bad air pollution that affects people's health. But like many cities, it also has an air-monitoring network. In recent years, smog alerts have closed factories and forced polluting cars off city streets. This has led some companies to clean up their production process and inhabitants to change their old cars for newer models that are more environmentally-friendly.

Smog alerts have helped to start the air clean-up process in places such as Mexico City.

Cooling the planet

Scientists believe air pollution is making the Earth hotter. The fight to stop this 'global warming' is a massive challenge – one that can only be won if everyone gets involved.

HEATING THE GREENHOUSE

The panes of glass in a greenhouse allow the Sun's rays in, but do not let all the heat out. Many gases in the atmosphere – especially carbon dioxide – act in the same way and are often called 'greenhouse gases' (see below). Recent human activity has made levels of greenhouse gases rise. That is why the Earth is thought to be heating up. This process is called global warming.

Countries in the developed world are a major source of carbon dioxide, produced by power stations such as this one. Some of these countries are leading the way in the fight against global warming.

atmosphere containing greenhouse gases

heat from the Sun

some heat is trapped and warms up the atmosphere

COOLING THE EARTH

About 100 countries have signed the Kyoto Agreement to reduce the amount of greenhouse gases the world produces. Carbon dioxide, for example, is produced when fossil fuels, such as coal and petrol, are used in power stations or cars. Most anti-global-warming action is therefore aimed at reducing the use of fossil fuels.

Global warming may raise the Earth's temperature by up to 5 degrees Celsius in the next 100 years. This could turn farmland like this into desert and destroy the habitats of many animals and plants.

Action stations

Copenhagen, the capital of Denmark, has pioneered a way of heating people's houses that uses as little energy as possible – and so causes less greenhouse gas production. Many houses in the city are kept warm by hot water that is piped from big boilers that serve whole districts. These 'district heating' systems are very energy efficient – much better than using electricity.

The city of Copenhagen aims to keep 'clean and green' by using less energy to heat its houses.

Car clean-up

Cars are the biggest source of air pollution in many cities around the world. Cars are widely used, so dealing with this problem is difficult. But new cleaner vehicles and better public transport systems are making a difference.

Traffic in the city of Cotonou in Benin, West Africa. The increase in car numbers worldwide is a massive pollution problem.

POLLUTION SOLUTIONS

Cars produce poisonous gases, such as nitrogen oxides, which contribute to air pollution. However, this pollution can be reduced by a catalytic converter or 'cat'. Most manufacturers fit cats to the exhausts of all new cars. Fuel-efficient engines also reduce the amount of carbon dioxide (the main greenhouse gas) cars produce.

Action stations

Singapore has kept the number of cars on its roads down by taxing cars heavily and by charging drivers to enter the city centre. The government has succeeded in getting people out of their cars and onto public transport, such as the city's ultra-modern train system, because it is reliable.

Travelling by train and other forms of public transport produces less carbon dioxide and other pollutants than travelling by car.

CLEANER TRANSPORT

Affordable, clean transport systems, such as light railways, are seen as an alternative to cars. In Curitiba, Brazil, buses provide easy-to-use, low-pollution transport for many people. In the Netherlands, most cities have a network of safe bicycle lanes, which encourage people to cycle.

This bus is one of many that run across Curitiba. Public transport systems like this are designed to reduce the use of cars.

Industry action

Factories cause a lot of pollution. But many companies around the world have found ways to make their factories meet strict laws, which limit the amount of air pollution they can produce.

CLEAN INDUSTRY

Controlling industrial pollution is vital. Pollution from industry can include heavy metals and other toxic chemicals. These can cause cancer and other life-threatening illnesses. To stop pollution escaping into the air, toxic chemicals are removed from factory chimneys by 'scrubbers'. However, this equipment is expensive and in poorer countries many companies either cannot afford them or do not fit them because there are no strict environmental laws.

To make sure companies meet strict anti-air-pollution laws factories are monitored closely. Unfortunately, not all countries have strict environmental laws.

CLEAN PRODUCTION

Air pollution can also be solved by not producing it in the first place. For example, many chemical companies are finding they can cut air pollution by changing how they make things and what raw materials they use. This 'clean production' approach can also help to save companies money because they do not need to pay to clean up any waste.

Action stations

Many companies are finding that cleaning up their factories brings other benefits. This has been shown by the Green Productivity Programme in Asia. Companies can reduce air pollution and save money by making their factories work better. One company in India involved in the programme cleaned up its air pollution and made savings of over US$300,000 a year.

Companies, like this tractor factory in India, can often get more customers by proving that they do not pollute the environment.

Clean power

Most electricity is made by power stations that burn fossil fuels such as coal, oil and gas. Worldwide, power stations produce a lot of air pollution – especially the old-fashioned ones that use coal.

A coal power station like this one (closed in 1983) helped to cause acid rain that polluted many lakes and rivers.

POLLUTING POWER

Burning coal, oil and gas to make electricity is a major source of carbon dioxide emissions. Energy production also causes over half of all emissions of sulphur dioxide – a gas that forms 'acid rain'. Since the early 1980s acid rain has killed fish in rivers and destroyed forests around the world.

CLEAN ENERGY

A lot has been done to make power stations cleaner. Since the mid-1980s Europe and North America have cut the sulphur dioxide pollution they produce by up to 80%. Clean, renewable ways of producing power, such as solar panels that convert energy from the Sun, are also becoming more widely used.

Renewable power, like that generated by solar panels, does not produce any air pollution or contribute to global warming.

Action stations

The best way to reduce the amount of pollution caused by power stations is to cut the amount of energy we use. You and your family can help by turning off electrical equipment, using energy-efficient light bulbs and by making sure that your house is properly insulated (so that it takes less energy to heat). The average UK household could stop the production of around two tonnes of carbon dioxide a year in this way.

Switching off a light when you don't need it on reduces the amount of energy you use, lowers air pollution and also cuts the price of fuel bills.

Chemical crackdown

Chemicals help us in many ways, but scientists have found out that some of them are very dangerous air pollutants. The worst ones are banned, but a lot of work remains to be done before the pollution risk is totally removed.

POPs

Scientists and environmental campaigners are very worried about chemicals called POPs (Persistent Organic Pollutants). POPs are hazardous chemicals, many of which were used or produced in a number of industrial processes, such as making electrical equipment. They last a long time and, if they leak into the environment, can be carried a great distance in the air. POPs have been linked with birth problems, disease and even death.

POPs are hazardous and have to be handled with extreme care. Many people believe that dangerous chemicals like these should be banned.

TOXIC BAN

A number of international agreements have been made to ban the worst POPs. However, some of these chemicals are still in use in the developing world and are released into the air when old products are broken down and burnt (see pages 24–25). Environmental campaign groups, such as Greenpeace, are demanding that the production of all dangerous POPs is stopped.

Dioxin – a by-product of many chemical processes, such as partial incineration – is one dangerous POP that is still produced.

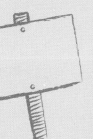

Action stations

Governments around the world have acted in the past to ban many dangerous chemicals. For example, in 1987 the Montreal Protocol was signed. This led to a ban on CFCs, chemicals that were used in aerosols and fridges, after it was discovered they damaged the ozone layer. This is a layer of ozone gas high in the atmosphere. It protects us from the dangerous ultraviolet rays produced by the Sun. Although it may still take many years before the ozone layer recovers, the CFC ban seems to have stopped its destruction.

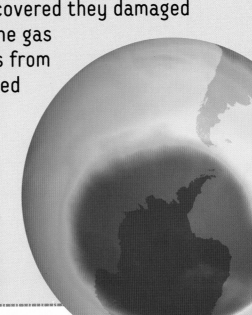

This photograph of the ozone layer was taken from space using a special satellite camera. The dark blue section over the South Pole shows the centre of the damage caused by CFCs.

Cleaning up indoors

The air inside houses and offices can get polluted and cause health problems, such as headaches, allergies and breathing difficulties. It is important to solve this problem because people are spending more time indoors.

POLLUTION INDOORS

Indoor air pollution comes from natural sources, such as mould, and from chemicals. These are given off by things such as cigarettes, paints, glues and faulty heating systems. If clean air does not get inside a building, pollutant levels can rise and cause health problems.

These specialists are removing a material called asbestos. It was banned after scientists discovered that people who breathe in asbestos fibres can develop cancer.

CLEANING INDOOR AIR

Indoor air pollution is usually easily solved. Finding and removing any pollutants is vital, but simply opening windows and letting fresh air in often helps. Certain types of house plant, such as the spider plant, can also filter and clean indoor air.

Plants not only make your house look nice – they can also help clean up air pollution.

Action stations

Some household products can release chemicals called Volatile Organic Compounds (VOCs), which are a source of indoor air pollution. However, there are alternatives that are not such a pollution risk. For example, low VOC or water-based paints give off less air pollution than normal oil-based types.

To stop indoor air pollution, use paints and other household products that contain low levels of VOCs.

New challenges

Some of the most important action against air pollution is taking place in the world's developing countries. There, old-fashioned factories, lack of money and poor law enforcement have often meant that air pollution is particularly bad.

OLYMPIC ACTION

China is one of the world's biggest producers of air pollution. Smoke from burning coal in its main cities has been linked to around 50,000 premature deaths a year. However, the Chinese authorities are acting to clean up the air. A local government scheme is improving air quality by reducing the emissions produced by power stations, cars and factories.

The Chinese capital, Beijing, celebrates its successful bid to host the Olympic Games in 2008. By then the city plans to have reduced pollution considerably, by cutting back the amount of coal that is burned. It will also improve public transport and close polluting factories.

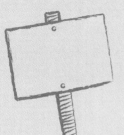

Action stations

One of the most worrying sources of air pollution in developing countries comes from hazardous waste. A lot of this was shipped from wealthier countries that paid to get rid of their waste. However, in the 1990s an important international law came into effect that has helped to stop this trade. The 'Basel Ban' made it illegal to export hazardous waste from rich to poor countries.

Greenpeace campaigns to stop the trade in hazardous waste. The trade has dropped significantly since the Basel Ban.

INDIAN TRANSPORT

Traffic emissions are a particular problem in developing world cities. Delhi, in India, is one of the world's most polluted cities. In an attempt to clean its air the city has bought a fleet of over 60,000 low-pollution buses, taxis and three-wheeled rickshaws that run on compressed natural gas.

Stop waste going up in smoke

Burning rubbish gets rid of waste but causes air pollution. New technology can help to limit these effects, but it is better to reduce the amount of waste we produce and stop the pollution happening in the first place.

RUBBISH PROBLEMS

Burning waste on open fires produces smoke and fumes. But even modern incinerators that burn rubbish at high temperatures have been linked with the production of dangerous POP chemicals (see pages 18–19). Even burying waste in the ground at landfill sites can cause air pollution. This is because as the rubbish rots away it produces methane, a greenhouse gas.

Smoke from the incinerator chimneys shown here creates air pollution. Campaign groups believe that we should recycle more so that less waste is burnt.

When you recycle, you reduce the amount of waste that goes to be incinerated or buried. This reduces air pollution.

ZERO WASTE

The best way to stop rubbish from producing air pollution is to make sure it does not get thrown away. In the USA, Europe and elsewhere, community recycling schemes make sure that materials, such as old metal, paper and plastic, are turned into new things, rather than being burnt or buried. Recycling materials helps to reduce the effects of global warming.

Action stations

Computers and other electronic machines contain a lot of chemicals, such as lead and mercury. These can create hazardous air pollution if they are not disposed of properly. Many of the world's leading computer manufacturers, such as IBM, now offer computer recycling services that aim to stop this happening.

Computers are just one of the many different kinds of waste that can be recycled to reduce pollution.

Fires and forests

Trees and forests are vital in the fight against air pollution. As trees grow they take in the greenhouse gas carbon dioxide. When forests burn they release this gas and produce a lot of other air pollutants.

Forest fires like this one produce air pollution that can seriously affect people's health, and even kill.

THE HAZE

In recent years there have been huge forest fires in many countries including Australia and France. In 1997 there was a giant forest fire in Indonesia that covered much of Southeast Asia in a choking haze. This affected the health of millions of people. To try and stop another disaster, the use of fire to clear land for farming has been banned.

SAVING TREES

In places around the world, such as South America and Asia, forests are cleared by people who want the land for farming or the wood for building. This causes a lot of air pollution. For many years, people have campaigned to stop the human destruction of ancient forests. Some campaigns have been successful; for example a large area of Canada's Great Bear Rainforest – the largest ancient temperate rainforest in the world – was recently saved from logging.

Trees are a very important way of dealing with air pollution because they take in carbon dioxide.

Action stations

A worldwide 'carbon trading' system is developing in which companies that produce carbon dioxide pay to have trees planted. The trees take in carbon dioxide, 'balancing' the pollution that the company itself makes. For example, a European electronics firm has paid to have millions of trees planted in Australia. This type of carbon trading could help plant giant new forests and reduce the effects of global warming.

Tree-planting schemes, like this one in Jamaica, help 'lock away' carbon dioxide as well as making a new home for animals and plants.

Communities clean up

Old pollution problems, such as London's smogs (see page 6), have been solved. But new problems, such as global warming, have appeared. Solving these problems will require action by communities all around the world.

A CHALLENGE FOR THE WORLD

As more people move to cities, cleaning up city air becomes ever more difficult. This is a particular problem in the developing world where there are rapidly growing 'mega-cities', with many millions of inhabitants. Many cities, such as those in East Asia and Australasia, are helping each other to clean up air pollution through schemes such as the World Bank's Clean Air Initiative (see www.worldbank.org/cleanair).

Cities like Sydney, Australia, where the air is relatively clean, have been helping more polluted cities in Asia with advice and expertise. The Clean Air Initiative encourages this sharing of knowledge.

PEOPLE POWER

People are working together as communities to stop air pollution by saving energy, taking public transport and recycling. In fact, air quality is the main focus of community work being done under the Local Agenda 21 global plan for action to improve the environment. This involves over 6,000 local governments and communities in over 100 countries.

We all have a part to play in keeping the air clean for the future, so that natural sights like this are not lost forever.

Action stations

Cleaning the air is something that everyone can play a part in. Here are four easy things you can do to help clean up the air: travel by bicycle or public transport when you can; plant a tree; switch off lights when a room is empty; and recycle. Find out what is happening in your community by contacting your local council to ask them what they are doing under Local Agenda 21 or their own local environmental plan.

Glossary

Acid rain Formed when sulphur dioxide and nitrogen oxides react in the atmosphere. Acid rain can make lakes acidic, hurt animals and plants and damage buildings.

Carbon dioxide The major greenhouse gas. Carbon dioxide is produced when fossil fuels are burned.

Catalytic converter (cat) A device fitted to a car that turns harmful exhaust gases into less toxic emissions.

CFCs Chemicals once used in aerosols and fridges, which are partly the cause of the destruction of the ozone layer.

Developed world The wealthier countries of the world, in which there are highly developed industries.

Developing world The poorer countries in the world, which rely more on farming than on industry.

Fossil fuels Fuels such as coal, gas or oil made from the fossilized remains of plants that lived millions of years ago. Burning fossil fuels produces the greenhouse gas carbon dioxide.

Global warming The gradual rise in the Earth's temperature.

Greenhouse effect The effect of various 'greenhouse' gases in the Earth's atmosphere that trap the heat of the Sun. Many greenhouse gases are made by human activities. Their increased production is thought to be raising global temperatures.

Greenhouse gases The gases that cause the greenhouse effect. The main ones are carbon dioxide, methane and CFCs.

Green productivity A way of running a company or business that combines reducing pollution with improving how products are made.

Hazardous waste Any waste (normally produced by industry) that is a hazard to the environment or to people's health.

Haze The name given to the visible air pollution that affects many countries.

Incineration The burning of industrial waste, domestic rubbish or other materials at high temperatures.

Lead A toxic metal produced by cars that do not run on unleaded petrol. High amounts of lead in the air are dangerous.

Nitrogen oxides Nitrogen oxides come from burning fossil fuels, in cars, lorries and power stations. They can make breathing problems worse. They also help form acid rain and ozone.

Ozone layer A thin layer of gas in the upper atmosphere that stops much of the Sun's ultraviolet rays (that can cause cancer) from reaching the Earth.

POPs Persistent Organic Pollutants. Long-lasting, hazardous chemicals that are used or produced in a number of industrial processes.

Smog Visible air pollution caused by gases from sources such as fires, factories, car engines and power stations.

Sulphur dioxide A gas mostly produced when coal or oil is burnt in power stations. It reacts in the atmosphere to form acid rain.

VOCs Volatile Organic Compounds, which come from many sources, including household products such as paint.

Find out more

www.greenpeace.org.uk Find out what Greenpeace is doing to combat air pollution and eliminate toxic chemicals from around the planet.

www.carbonneutralnewcastle.com Click on this site to find out what the city of Newcastle upon Tyne in the UK is doing to reduce the amount of carbon dioxide it is producing.

www.eco-schools.org.uk Lots of information about what your school can do to combat air pollution – and what you can do while you are at, or travelling to, your classroom.

www.epa.gov/students/air.htm Visit this site for information about indoor air pollution, ozone, smog, acid rain and many other air pollution topics from the organisation that protects the USA's environment.

www.globalactionplan.org.uk The site of an exciting project that gets families involved in really positive projects to help the environment. Check out the pollution-busting projects in the transport and energy sections. Why not ask your parents to sign up to the scheme?

Index